This Books Belongs To.........

....

....

....

Trace the steps for making the letter a on the following line.

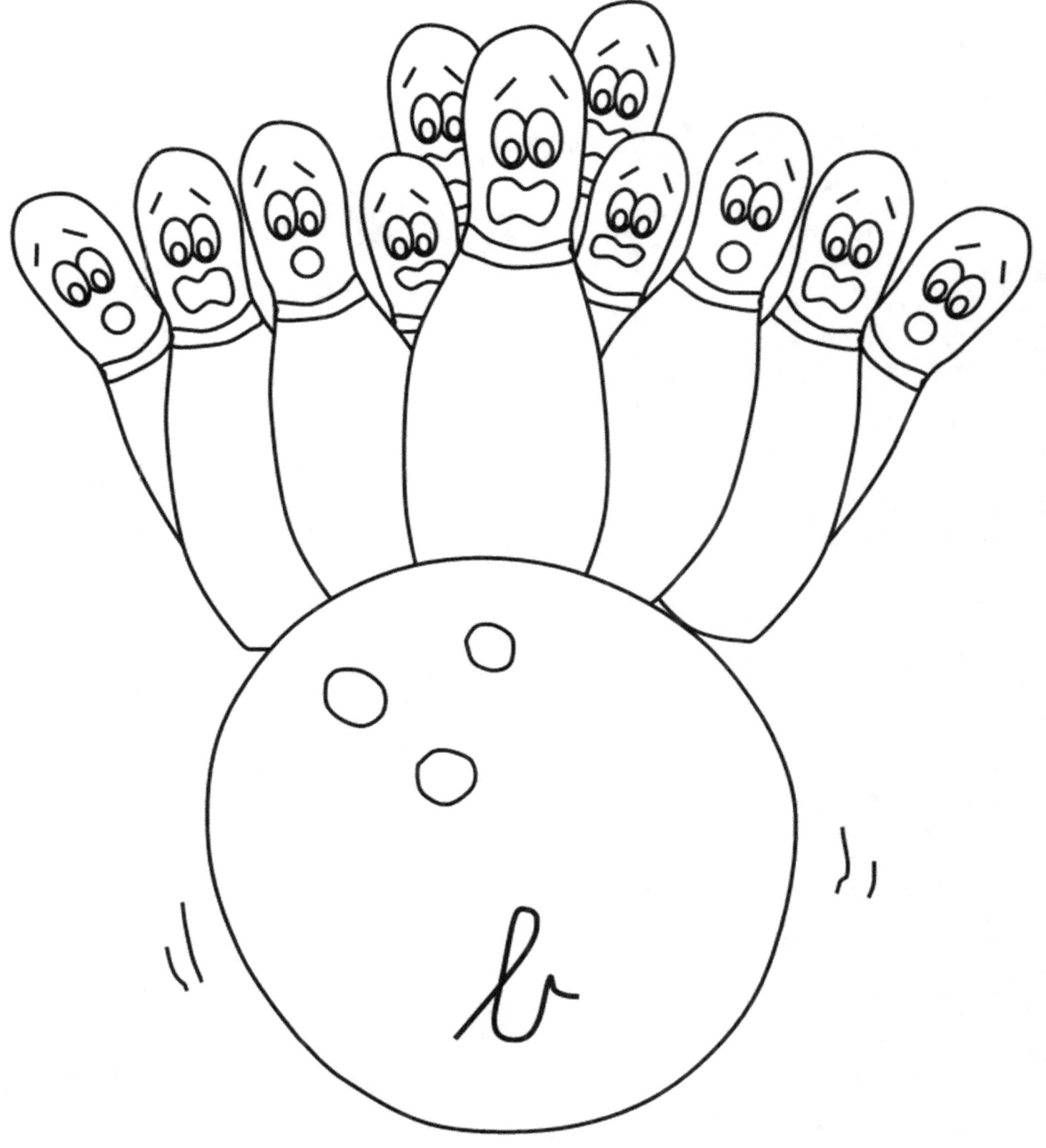

Trace the steps for making the letter b on the following line.

Trace the steps for making the letter c on the following line.

Trace the steps for making the letter c on the following line.

c *h* *ch* *ch* *ch* *ch*

Trace the steps for making the letter d on the following line.

d   d   d   d   d   d   d   dd

Trace the steps for making the letter e on the following line.

Trace the steps for making the letter f on the following line.

Trace the steps for making the letter g on the following line.

Trace the steps for making the letter h on the following line.

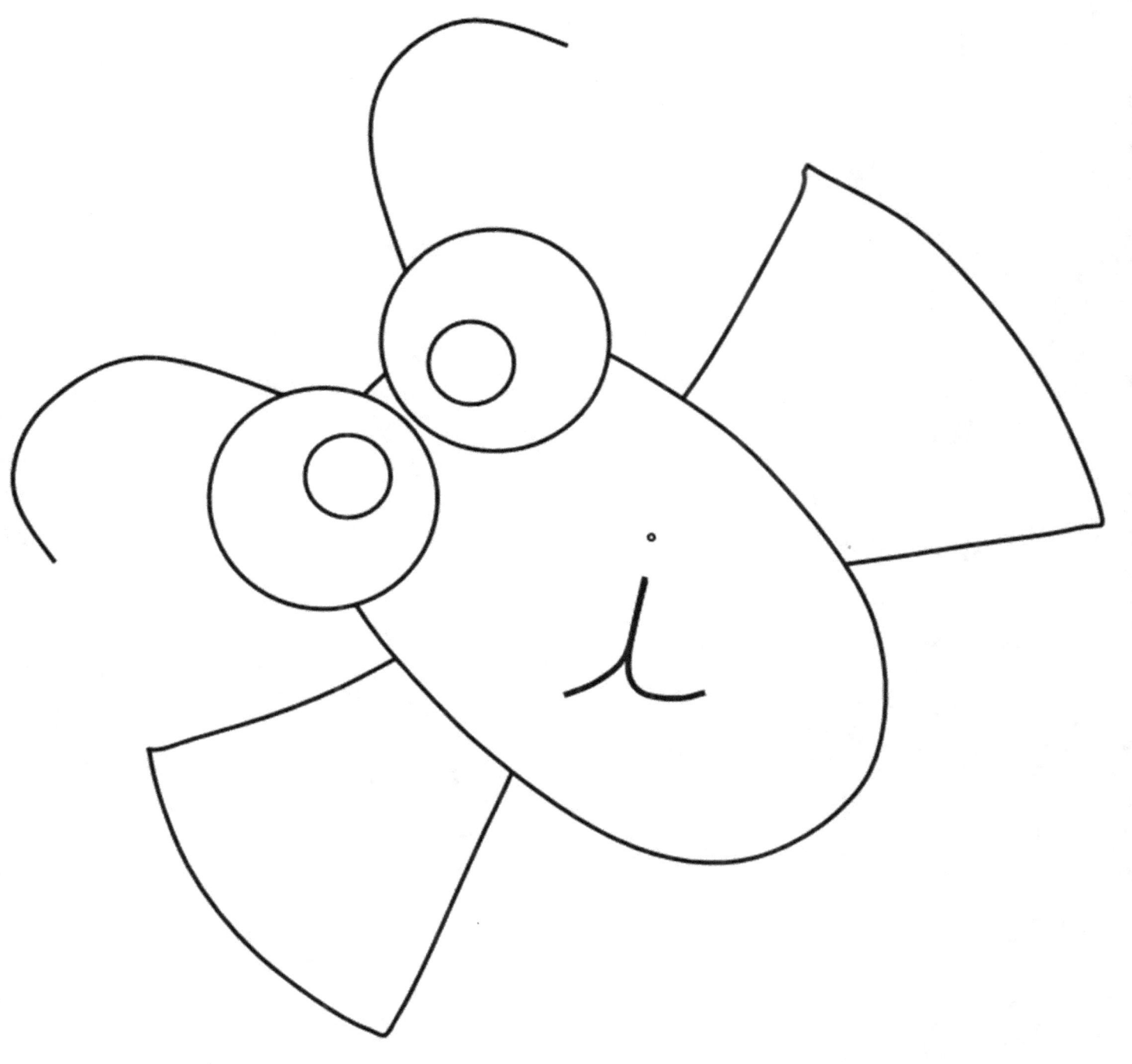

Trace the steps for making the letter i on the following line.

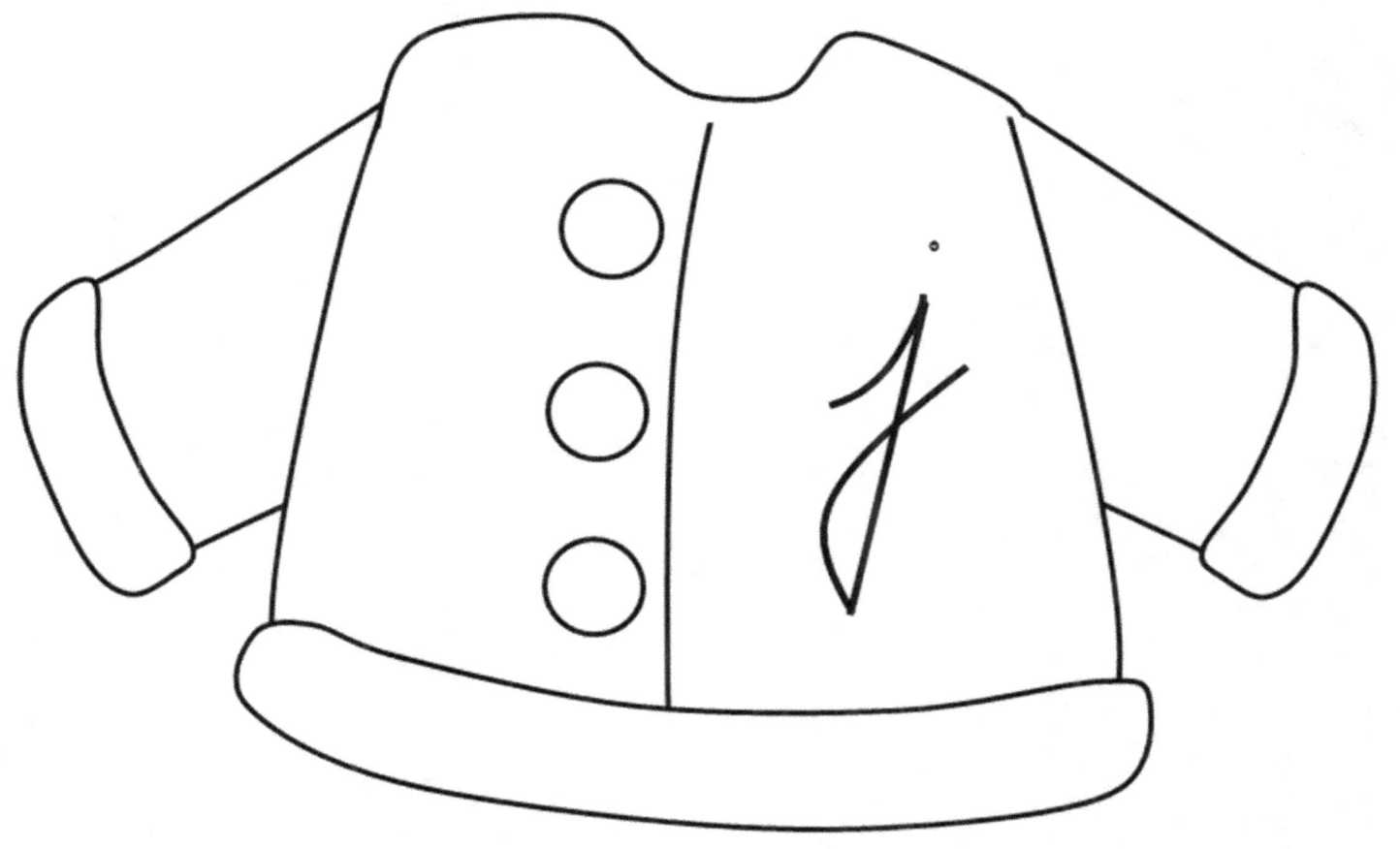

Trace the steps for making the letter j on the following line.

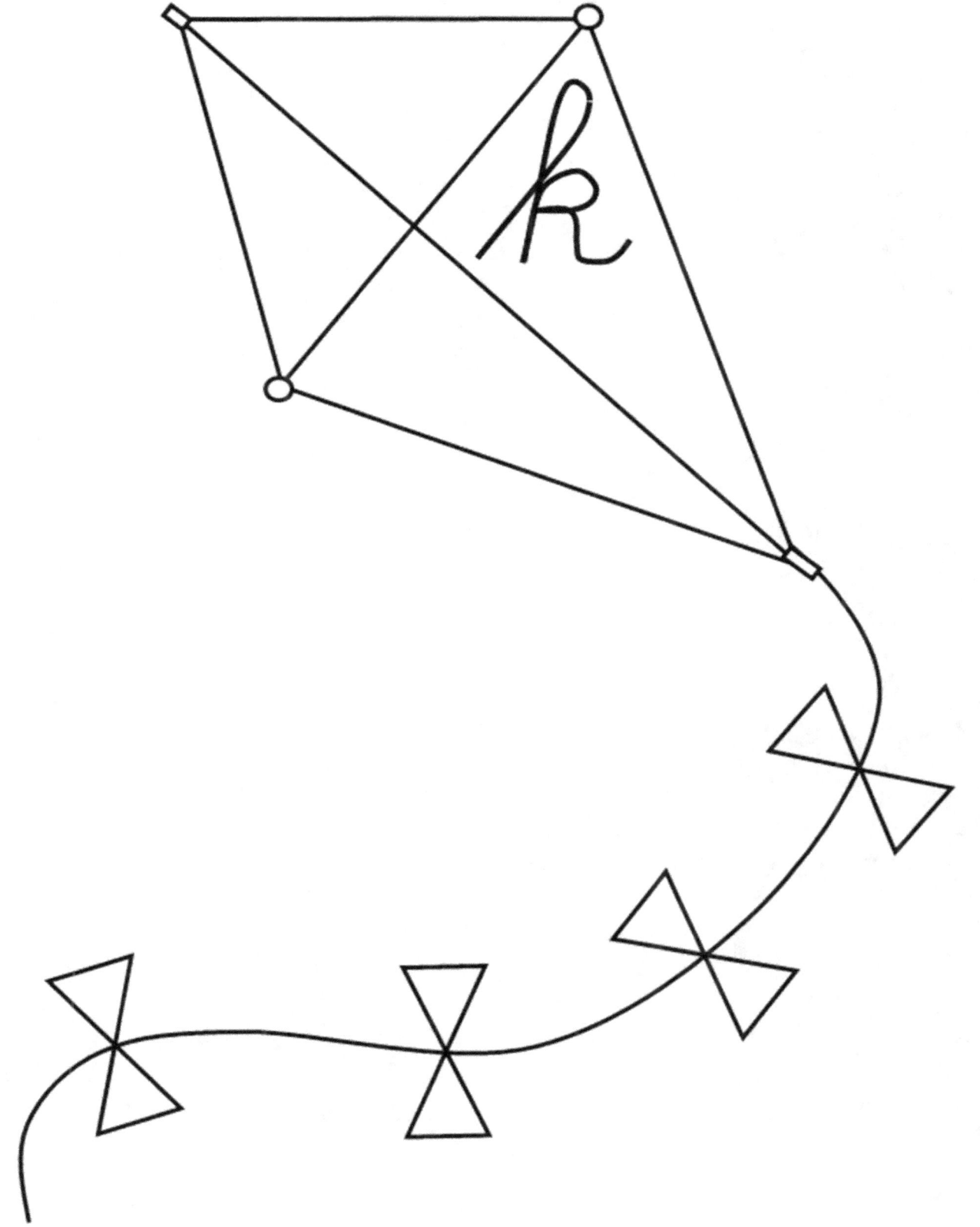

Trace the steps for making the letter k on the following line.

Trace the steps for making the letter l on the following line.

Trace the steps for making the letter m on the following line.

_____

J J JM JM JM JM JM JM JM

Trace the steps for making the letter n on the following line.

_____

⌐⌐ ⌐⌐ n n n n n n n n n

Trace the steps for making the letter o on the following line.

Trace the steps for making the letter p on the following line.

p p p p p p pp

Trace the steps for making the letter q on the following line.

Trace the steps for making the letter r on the following line.

_____
‾ ‾

Trace the steps for making the letter s on the following line.

Trace the steps for making the letter sh on the following line.

s   h   sh   sh   sh   sh

Trace the steps for making the letter t on the following line.

Th

Trace the steps for making the letter th on the following line.

t   h   th   th   th   th

Trace the steps for making the letter u on the following line.

Trace the steps for making the letter v on the following line.

Trace the steps for making the letter w on the following line.

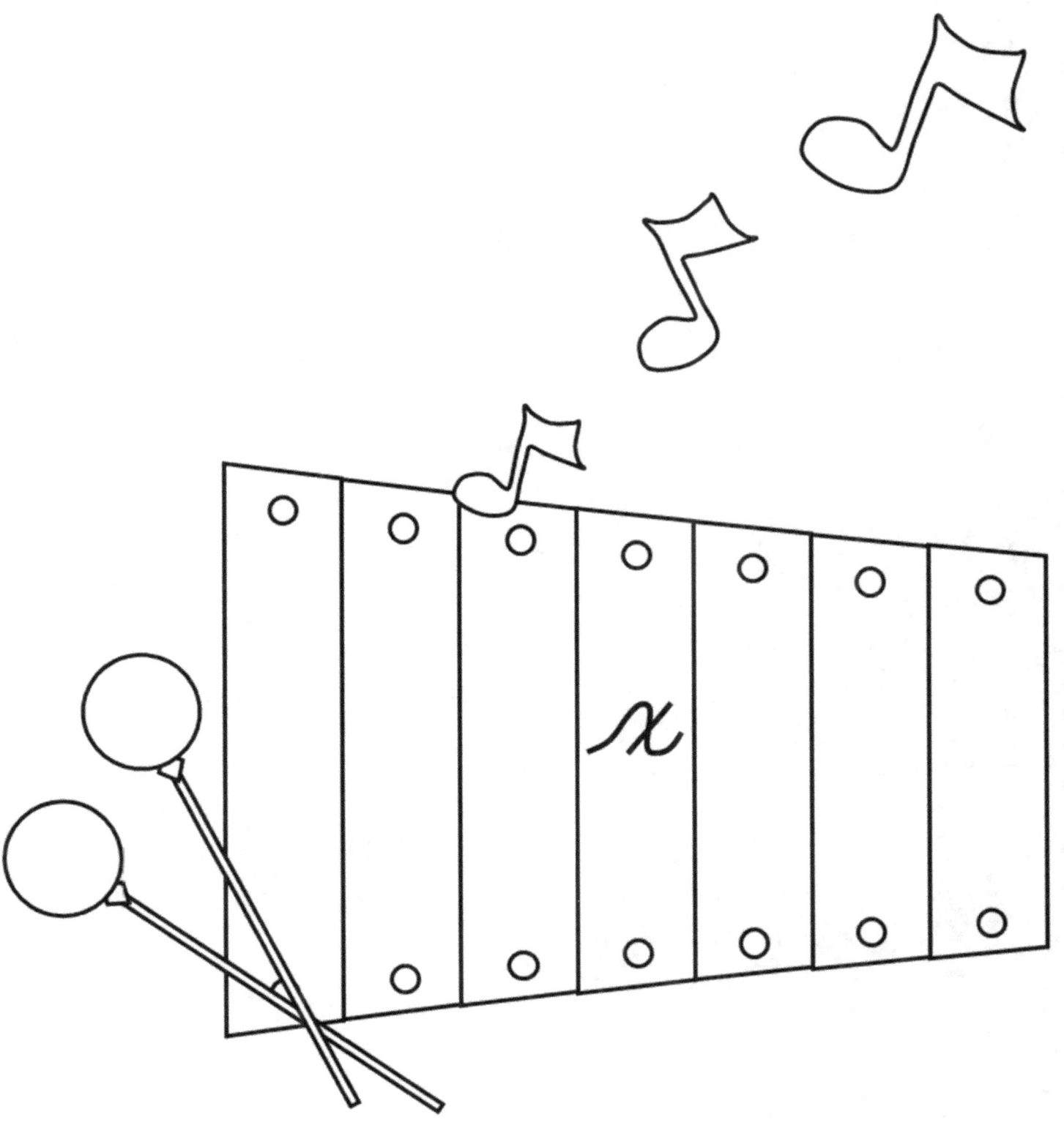

Trace the steps for making the letter x on the following line.

Trace the steps for making the letter y on the following line.

Trace the steps for making the letter z on the following line.